MONSTER TRUCKS

Paul Mason

First published in 2009
by Franklin Watts

Copyright © Franklin Watts 2009

Franklin Watts
338 Euston Road
London NW1 3BH

Franklin Watts Australia
Level 17/207 Kent Street
Sydney, NSW 2000

Planning and production by
Tall Tree Limited
Editor: Rob Colson
Designer: Jonathan Vipond

Dewey number 629.224

ISBN 978 0 7496 8695 6

Printed in China

Franklin Watts is a division of Hachette Children's
Books, an Hachette UK company.

www.hachette.co.uk

CONTENTS

MONSTER RACING

As the crowd sits waiting for the first monster truck race to begin, all conversation stops. It has to – no one can hear over the noise of the **revving** engines! The start signal goes and the trucks leap away from the line – they're off!

WHAT IS A MONSTER TRUCK?

Monster trucks are giant pick-up trucks, with huge wheels and very tall **suspension**. They are so high off the ground that you need a ladder to climb up to the driver's seat. The trucks are designed to be able to drive over almost any obstacle.

▽ *The USAF Afterburner showing the massive tyres, wheels and suspension fitted to monster trucks.*

MONSTER TRUCK RACING

In monster truck racing, two trucks set off side-by-side from the start line. The racetrack is like an obstacle course. The trucks drive over cars, leap off ramps and make tight turns. The aim is to be the first to cross the finish line. The winning truck goes through to the next round.

▷ *The Eradicator gets airborne off a ramp during a Monster Jam racing event at Miami in February 2008.*

FREESTYLE

Monster truck events often finish with a freestyle display. Freestyle is like a dance routine for trucks. They rear up on their back wheels and do spins and other tricks. The highlight of the freestyle display is often when the truck crushes an old caravan or motorhome.

TECHNICAL DATA

Amazingly for such big vehicles, monster trucks are great at jumping. In 1999, Dan Runte set a world record of 61.5 metres by jumping Bigfoot 14 over a Boeing 727 passenger jet. This record was set at Smyrna Airport, Tennessee, USA.

HISTORY OF MONSTER TRUCKS

Monster truck racing is one of the newest kinds of motorsport. The first monster truck was built in the 1970s. The truck made its debut appearance at a car show in 1979, and in the 1980s the idea of monster truck competitions came about.

BIGFOOT – THE FIRST MONSTER TRUCK

The first monster truck was called Bigfoot. In 1981, a **promoter** saw a film of Bigfoot crushing old cars in a field. He asked Bigfoot's owner and builder, Bob Chandler, to repeat the event for an audience. Chandler agreed, and in 1982 the first-ever monster truck car crush was held.

△ *Bigfoot flies over cars during a monster truck rally at Anaheim Stadium in California.*

NEW MONSTER TRUCKS

Bigfoot was so popular that Bob Chandler was forced to build another one. Now Bigfoot could appear in two places at once. Other car-crushing monster trucks began to appear. Bear Foot, King Kong and the Virginia Giant were among the rivals for Bigfoot's crown.

▽ Monster trucks do not only appear in giant events. At this small monster truck rally, an oversized truck drives over wrecked cars to amaze the crowd.

COMPETITION

The monster-truck builders were constantly trying to outdo each other. They all wanted the biggest, tallest, longest and heaviest truck. They kept adding bigger wheels, tyres and engines. The trucks became huge, and the biggest trucks of today dwarf the original monsters.

▽ Children stand in the giant wheels of Bigfoot 5.

TECHNICAL DATA

Bigfoot 5 was built in 1986, using 3 metre tall tyres that had belonged to the US Army in the 1950s. When it appeared, Bigfoot 5 became the world's tallest (4.7 metre), widest (6.3 metre) and heaviest (17,000 kg) monster truck.

MONSTER TRUCK TRACKS

Monster truck racing grew up in the USA, but today it is also popular elsewhere. Big crowds are drawn to both indoor and outdoor races in Canada and Europe. And of course, TV coverage of monster truck events is beamed into living rooms around the world.

CARS – THE ORIGINAL OBSTACLE

Car crushing was what originally made monster trucks popular. When monster trucks began to race each other, the race was to see who could roll over a line of cars the quickest. Today, every monster truck racecourse has at least one set of cars for the trucks to roll over.

▽ *Monster trucks often rear up on their back wheels, before smashing down on a line of cars.*

RAMPS AND BARRIERS

As well as cars, monster truck racetracks often have dirt ramps. These are steep on one side and shallow on the other. The trucks have to jump over them. Often there are cars or vans behind the ramp for the truck to crush or leap.

▽ A monster truck jumps over a line of vehicles. In races, trucks aim to get round the course as fast as possible. They take the jumps at speed.

TIGHT TURNS AND SAVES

Monster trucks can turn in a tiny area because all four wheels can turn together. As it speeds around a corner, a truck's inner wheels often lift up into the air. It seems impossible for it to stay upright. When it does stay upright, the driver gets a big cheer for making a 'save'.

TECHNICAL DATA

A crew of eight workers usually takes about three days, working 18–20 hours a day, to build a monster truck course. About 2,675 cubic metres of dirt is used to build a large course.

DRIVING A MONSTER TRUCK

Imagine what it's like racing a monster truck. Just sitting in the cab, you're as high up as a first floor window. So how do you get to start the engine and actually drive one of these giant vehicles in a competition?

GETTING A RACE LICENCE

If you want to race a monster truck, you need a race licence! To get one, you must show that you can safely control a truck as it crushes or jumps cars. Once you have done this at ten different events, the other drivers may award you a Class A racing licence.

◁ In many trucks, the driver sits in the middle of the cab for the best possible **visibility**.

STEERING THE TRUCK

Trucks can be steered in a variety of ways, even using a joystick like that in a helicopter! Usually, a steering wheel controls the front wheels, and a lever on the **dashboard** steers the rear wheels. Steering is powered using high-pressure liquid – a system called hydraulics.

△ The Grave Digger takes a tight corner with all four wheels turning to get the monster truck around in time.

TECHNICAL DATA

The **axles** (the metal rods connecting the front or back wheels) of many monster trucks originally came from either military vehicles or old school buses!

OTHER CONTROLS

Drivers control the truck's speed by pressing down on the accelerator pedal to speed up, or the brake pedal to slow down. Sometimes a control allows the driver to add extra fuel to the engine. This boosts the truck's power for a short burst of speed.

ENGINES AND GEARS

Modern racing monster trucks aren't really trucks at all! They're actually more like giant, scaled-up dune buggies. Most of them have a lightweight pickup-shaped body, but only because the first monster trucks were **modified** pickup trucks.

ENGINES

Monster truck engines are specially built. They're about six times as big as a normal car's, and are usually **supercharged** and run on **methanol**. Monster trucks are not very fuel-efficient. They burn about 11 litres of fuel in every 75-metre run. A normal family car could travel over 150 km on the same amount of fuel.

SPEED VERSUS POWER

Top speed is not important, but the trucks need lots of power in very short bursts. As the truck's front wheels hit a car and lift up, the driver accelerates. The back wheels drive forwards and the truck rears up before coming crashing down on the car.

△ With a burst of power to all four wheels, Shattered soars over a line of crushed cars at the Qualcomm Stadium, San Diego, USA, in January 2009.

GEARBOXES

A lot happens in a monster truck race. Drivers have to watch their opponent, steer the front and back wheels, and control the power – they have plenty to think about without needing to change gear as well! Fortunately they do not need to, because most trucks are **automatics**.

◄ As Big Foot accelerates away from a standing start, the truck squats down on its rear wheels and rears up at the front.

TECHNICAL DATA

The cars that are crushed during monster truck events usually come from local junkyards. They are returned once the racing is over – already part-crushed! The Monster Jam monster truck series alone crushes about 3,000 cars a year.

CHASSIS, SUSPENSION AND TYRES

The first thing you notice about a monster truck is how big its tyres are. Those giant tyres put a big strain on the rest of the truck. Every part has to be beefed up to cope with the extra effort of turning and steering them.

▷ The Grave Digger rides on massive 1.7-metre tyres. Its huge suspension needs to cope with the impact of a 30-metre jump.

CHASSIS

The chassis is the framework that holds the truck together. Modern monster truck chassis are specially made out of steel tubing. The engine is usually mounted to the chassis behind the driver's cab. The suspension attaches near the corners.

SUSPENSION

Monster trucks absorb some big bumps – so they need big suspension. Their **long-travel suspension** allows the tyre to move up and down by as much as 1.2 metres. The trucks sway left, right, forward and backward, like someone who has stood up too quickly and is feeling a bit dizzy.

TECHNICAL DATA

*Most monster trucks use **shock absorbers** (shocks) filled with nitrogen gas. The trucks weigh 4,000–5,450 kg, so the shocks have a lot of work to do. Some trucks even use two shocks per wheel to absorb the weight.*

TYRES

Monster trucks often use giant 'terra' tyres, which are also used on the biggest **combine harvesters**. Some race series require a specific size of tyre. The tyres are specially adapted to suit different tracks by cutting their surface. Cutting a single tyre can take 50 hours!

SAFETY FEATURES

Monster trucks are designed to be able to drive over almost anything. Even so, once in a while the driver loses control, and a truck may flip right over onto its back. Modern trucks have a range of safety features to keep the drivers and spectators safe.

CROWD SAFETY

If a monster truck went on the rampage through the crowd, it could cause serious injuries. Fortunately, all race trucks have a **kill switch**. The driver flips this to stop the engine if the truck runs out of control. A safety marshal at the side of the track has a remote-control kill switch as a backup.

▽ *Hot Wheels monster truck flips over during a show. In this situation, a kill switch cuts power to the fuel pump and ignition system, stopping the engine and preventing a fire.*

TRUCK SAFETY FEATURES

Monster trucks are fitted with **roll cages** in case they turn over. If there is a fire, onboard fire extinguisher systems help to put it out. Fire barriers protect the driver. Shields make sure that if the engine blows up, pieces cannot fly out and injure anyone.

TECHNICAL DATA

Drivers are kept in their seats by a five-point harness. The harness's straps come from over each shoulder, from each side and from between the legs, and connect to a central clip.

DRIVER SAFETY EQUIPMENT

Drivers are well protected in their seats. They wear a safety harness to stop them being thrown around inside the cab. In addition, each race driver wears a fireproof suit, helmet, eye protection and a **HANS** device or neck brace.

△ *To prevent debris flying off a rolling monster truck, moving parts are surrounded in tough casing. Some parts also have safety straps to keep them in place.*

MONSTER TRUCK RACING

Monster truck racing must be the only motorsport where the vehicles are more popular than the drivers. The crowds cheer for their favourite trucks and boo their rivals. No wonder some people say that monster truck racing is the motorsports version of professional wrestling!

INTRODUCING THE RACERS

At the start of the event, the lights go down. The drivers are introduced one by one. A spotlight shines down on them as they climb on to their trucks. Each group of fans tries to give their favourite the biggest cheer of the night.

▼ The Bounty Hunter roars away from the starting line around a track laid with bales of hay.

STARTING THE RACE

The first two trucks roll to the start line, revving their engines. The starter stands in front of them and raises a flag. As soon as the flag drops, the drivers hit the accelerator. (Sometimes red and green start lights are used instead.) The race is on!

△ An official holds up a green flag to show to the driver of the Dragon Slayer that it's clear to race.

TECHNICAL DATA

Monster truck racing is expensive! On average, a truck gets through five engines a year – each engine costs almost £25,000. Each body shell costs about £35,000 when new, and another £2,000 every time it has to be rebuilt. And the tyres cost nearly £2,000 each!

TRUCK AGAINST TRUCK

The drivers have only one aim – to get to the finish line first. The loser leaves the contest and the winner goes through to the next round. In the end, only two trucks are left. These last two race to decide the winner.

FREESTYLE

Imagine going to a monster truck event, then seeing your favourite truck knocked out in the first round! Fortunately, today monster truck fans get a second chance to see their favourites – in the freestyle section.

▽ *Monster Mutt catches some air over a line of vehicles during a freestyle display at Tampa, Florida, USA.*

FREESTYLE COMPETITION

Today, freestyle events are often competitions. The trucks have a set time to perform as many tricks as possible. Usually, three judges fill out scorecards and their scores are added together to decide the result. Sometimes the crowd gets to decide – an 'applause-o-meter' measures which truck gets the loudest cheer.

MODERN FREESTYLE

Freestyle displays are like a stunt show for the trucks. They give the drivers a chance to show what their trucks can do, including tricks that would slow them down in a race.

Among the most popular freestyle tricks are long jumps, high jumps, different kinds of wheelie and spinning turns called donuts. The grand finale of a freestyle event is nearly always a monster truck destroying a motorhome or caravan.

△ *A truck driver greets the crowds at the end of another successful freestyle competition.*

MONSTER TRUCK COMPETITIONS

Monster trucks are most popular in the USA and Europe, where different organisations run events. The smallest events feature four or five trucks, but the biggest can have as many as 15 or more. Big events are often held in sports stadiums and attract massive crowds.

MONSTER JAM

The **USHRA**'s Monster Jam (see page 28) probably runs more monster truck contests than anyone else. In 2004, over 3 million people went to USHRA events. There are events all year, but the main competition season runs from January to March. The season's finale is the Monster Jam World Finals, held at the end of March.

▽ *Batman has one of the most customised bodies in the Monster Jam arena. Huge fins stick out of the jet-black body.*

MONSTER JAM EUROPE AND CANADA

In Europe, the Monster Jam season runs through summer and autumn. There are events in a variety of countries: in 2008, Monster Jam visited Britain, Sweden (twice), Denmark, Belgium, Holland, Spain and Finland. That same year, the world's biggest monster truck series also held seven events in Canada.

▷ *The US Air Force promotes itself around the world with the help of its Afterburner monster truck.*

TECHNICAL DATA

MONSTER JAM WORLD CHAMPIONS

	RACING	*FREESTYLE*
2000	Goldberg (Tom Meents)	Grave Digger (Dennis Anderson)
2001	Goldberg (Tom Meents)	Goldberg (Tom Meents)
2002	Team Meents (Tom Meents)	Team Meents (Tom Meents)
2003	Wolverine (Brian Barthel)	Avenger (Jim Koehler)
2004	Grave Digger (Dennis Anderson)	Maximum Destruction (Tom Meents)
2005	Madusa (Debra Miceli)	Bounty Hunter (Jimmy Creten)
2006	Grave Digger (Dennis Anderson)	Maximum Destruction (Tom Meents)
2007	Batman (John Seasock)	Captain's Curse (Pablo Huffaker)
2008	Batman (John Seasock)	Taz (Adam Anderson)
2009	Maximum Destruction (Tom Meents)	Air Force Afterburner (Damon Bradshaw)

FAMOUS TRUCKS

Monster truck racing has plenty of famous drivers, but most audiences come to see the trucks themselves! Race fans recognise their favourites immediately and even give them personalities. Some trucks are goodies and one or two are baddies.

Bigfoot was the first monster truck and is probably still the most famous. There have been many different versions of Bigfoot: by 2008, 23 Bigfoots had been built. Some are now just display vehicles, but many are still active race trucks.

△ Maximum Destruction, driven by monster truck legend Tom Meents, whose previous drives included Monster Patrol and Bulldozer.

GRAVE DIGGER

Grave Digger is probably the most popular monster truck in the world. The first version of Grave Digger was based on a 1951/2 pickup truck. It got its name when Grave Digger's builder, Dennis Anderson, told another racer: "I'll take this old junk and dig you a grave with it."

△ As well as the body of an old pickup truck, Dennis Anderson used bits and pieces from other scrapped vehicles to create the first Grave Digger.

TECHNICAL DATA

Monster trucks have their own secret language. Here are three popular phrases:

• "Mash the motor" = accelerate.

• "Endo" = spectacular, end-over-end crash.

• "Sky wheelie" = truck rears up on its rear wheels so that it is pointing straight up in the air.

MAXIMUM DESTRUCTION

Maximum Destruction was originally called Goldberg, after a famous heavyweight wrestler called Bill Goldberg. In 2003, it was renamed Maximum Destruction. The truck is very tough and regularly shrugs off big crashes. It is also famous for doing big jumps.

GLOSSARY

automatics
Vehicles that change gear automatically.

axles
Metal rods connecting the front or back wheels together.

cabin switches
Controls inside the cabin of a truck.

combine harvesters
Giant machines for harvesting crops such as corn.

dashboard
Display panel in front of a vehicle's driver, which shows speed, engine revs and other information.

donuts
Tight spins, where the front of the truck stays in place while the rear wheels skid around it.

HANS
Short for Head And Neck Safety device.

kill switch
Switch that stops (or 'kills') the engine when the truck is flipped.

long-travel suspension
Suspension that allows the wheel to move up and down a long way.

methanol
A fuel made from wood or other plants.

modified
Altered or changed.

promoter
Person who puts on shows or events in the hope of selling tickets.

revving
Making the engine roar by pushing and releasing the accelerator.

roll cage
Extra-strong metal framework that cannot be crushed if a vehicle rolls over.

shock absorbers
Telescopic tubes that shorten to absorb bumps.

slap wheelies
Using the bounce after a jump to lift a truck's front wheels into the air.

supercharged
Able to draw extra gases into the engine, giving it more power.

suspension
Mechanical device or devices that absorb bumps as a vehicle moves on a surface.

USHRA
Short for United States Hot Rod Association.

visibility
Ability to see clearly in every direction.

STAR DRIVERS

TOM MEENTS

Born: 10 July 1967
Nationality: American

Eight times world champion, Meents is famous for his full-throttle driving style, which ensures Maximum Destruction regularly crashes! In Sweden in 2007, he became the first person to do a 360 degree backflip in a monster truck.

DENNIS ANDERSON

Born: 24 October 1960
Nationality: American

Anderson's first monster truck win was in 1986, when his truck Grave Digger beat Bigfoot. Anderson won the first freestyle world championship in 2000 – and was followed by his son Adam, who won the championship in 2008.

DEBRA MICELI

Born: 9 February 1964
Nationality: American (born in Italy)

Miceli first became famous as a pro wrestler. She is one of very few women to make an impact in monster truck driving. She won the 2004 freestyle world championship and the 2005 racing world championship. Miceli now drives for Team Bigfoot.

JOE CYPHER

Born: 14 January 1964
Nationality: New Zealander

Cypher is an amazing character: the first (and so far only) disabled monster truck driver. Unable to use his legs after a car accident, he produced a truck that can be driven using hand controls only, and became a top monster truck racer.

JOHN SEASOCK

Born: 3 July 1965
Nationality: American

In recent years, Seasock has been almost unbeatable at the world championships, racing T-Maxx to victory in 2007 and 2008. He is also known for his charity work, in particular for hospitals and schools.

JIM KOEHLER

Born: 13 July 1966
Nationality: American

Koehler's dynamic freestyle moves, added to his occasional wild crashes, have made him a firm favourite at Monster Jam events. He drives a truck called Avenger.

WEBSITES

www.monsterjamonline.com/home
The home page of the largest monster truck racing organisation. There's lots going on here, though it's not always that easy to find. There are excellent sections with features on the trucks and drivers, and the site is a great way to find the nearest Monster Jam event to you.

www.bigfoot4x4.com
"The official website for the original monster truck," it says on the first page, and that's exactly what this is. The 'History and FAQ' page is especially interesting.

www.monstertrucks.net
A webpage packed with links to other sites on monster trucks, races, events and organisations.

www.mtra.us
The website of the Monster Truck Racing Association. Created in 1987, the MTRA formulates the rules followed by Monster Truck teams and ensures that safety rules are strictly followed.

Please note: every effort has been made by the Publishers to ensure that these websites contain no inappropriate or offensive material. However, because of the nature of the Internet, it is impossible to guarantee that the contents of these sites will not be altered. We strongly advise that Internet access is supervised by a responsible adult.

INDEX